Scaredy Bat

and the Art Thief

By Marina J. Bowman

Illustrated by Paula Vrinceanu

CODE
PINEAPPLE

First paperback edition July 2022

Written by Marina J. Bowman
Illustrated by Paula Vrinceanu
Book Design by Emy Farella

ISBN 978-1-950341-61-0 (paperback black & white)
ISBN 978-1-950341-62-7 (paperback color)
ISBN 978-1-950341-63-4 (ebook)

Published by Code Pineapple
www.codepineapple.com

For those who find the light, even in the darkest of times.

Also by
Marina J. Bowman

SCAREDY BAT

A supernatural detective series for kids with courage, teamwork, and problem solving. If you like solving mysteries and overcoming fears, you'll love this enchanting tale!

#1 Scaredy Bat and the Frozen Vampires
#2 Scaredy Bat and the Sunscreen Snatcher
#3 Scaredy Bat and the Missing Jellyfish
#4 Scaredy Bat and the Haunted Movie Set
#5 Scaredy Bat and the Mega Park Mystery
#6 Scaredy Bat and the Art Thief
Scaredy Bat and the Holiday Mysteries
Hailey Haddie's Minute Mysteries

THE LEGEND OF PINEAPPLE COVE

A fantasy-adventure series for kids with bravery, kindness, and friendship. If you like reimagined mythology and animal sidekicks, you'll love this legendary story!

#1 Poseidon's Storm Blaster
#2 A Mermaid's Promise
#3 King of the Sea
#4 Protector's Pledge

Free
Minute Mystery
Short Story

As a gift, we'd like to send you a FREE Minute Mystery called

"The Case of the Leaping Laboratory" so you can continue the mystery-solving fun!

GO HERE TO GET

YOUR FREE MINUTE MYSTERY NOW:

scaredybat.com/book6

Detective Team

Jessica
"the courage"

Ellie
aka Scaredy Bat
"the detective"

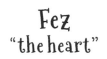

Fez
"the heart"

Tink
"the brains"

Contents

Batty Bonuses

Can you solve the mystery?

All you need is an eye for detail, a sharp memory, and good logical skills. Join Ellie on her mystery-solving adventure by making a suspect list and figuring out who committed the crime! To help with your sleuthing, you'll find a suspect list template and hidden details observation sheets at the back of the book.

There's a place not far from here
With strange things 'round each corner
It's a town where vampires walk the streets
And unlikely friendships bloom

When there's a mystery to solve
Ellie Spark is the vampire to call
Unless she's scared away like a cat
Poof! There goes that Scaredy Bat

Villains and pesky sisters beware
No spider, clown, or loud noise
Will stop Ellie and her team
From solving crime, one fear at a time

Chapter 1
Hide-and-Seek

Creak. Crack. Creak.

The wood stairs groaned as Ellie Spark raced to the attic. With each step, the smell of paint and stale coffee strengthened.

"Eighteen, nineteen, twenty!" came Penny's voice from downstairs. "Ready or not, here I come!"

Sketches and newspaper clippings on a bulletin board flapped and crinkled as Ellie zipped past them. She quickly shoved the whiny rolling chair out from under the long wooden desk. As she tried to squish herself where the seat was, the smell of bubblegum filled her nose. She sniffed the air, tracking the aroma to right above her head. A mosaic of colorful gobs of gum decorated the underside

of the desk.

"Ew, Penny," Ellie whispered. Her little sister was always chewing gum when she colored in the attic art studio. Apparently, those chewy morsels were not making it to the garbage. Ellie unstuck one of her long brown strands from a green gob and sought out a less sticky hiding spot.

Creak. Crack. Creak.

Her heart raced at the sound of footsteps on the stairs. She jammed herself behind a red dresser, desperate to not be found by her little sister. After all, this was one game of hide-and-seek she didn't want to lose. The loser owed the winner their portion of dessert all next week. And Ellie was not willing to give up her favorite food ever—ooey gooey blood pudding. She tried to squash herself further behind the dresser, but no matter how hard she squeezed her legs in, her moon socks poked out. She scrambled back to her feet.

Creak. Crack. Creak.

She bolted to the closet, whipping an empty easel with her long turquoise trench coat. It fell

to the floor with a *BANG!*

Creak. Crack. Creak.

Out of time, she left the downed easel and dove into the closet jammed with musty old clothes. She tried to quiet her breathing as she peeked through the crack in the door.

Mrs. Spark appeared at the top of the stairs with a fistful of clean paint brushes. Her messy bun bobbed along to whatever tune was blasting through her headphones. She hummed as she stuffed the brushes into the red dresser. Ever since dropping off her painting for the museum's art exhibit, she had been in a great mood.

Ellie let out a sigh of relief. Her eyes trailed the floor-length curtains across the room gently swaying in the breeze. Deciding that would be a much better—and less cramped—hiding spot, she quietly pushed the door open.

Creak. Crack. Creak.

Ellie pulled the closet door shut, once again leaving a small crack to squint through. Penny poked her head into the attic and scanned the studio.

"Mom, have you seen Ellie?" she asked.

Mrs. Spark continued to hum as she organized the drawers.

"Mom?" Penny repeated. "MOM?"

Instead of answering, Mrs. Spark's humming turned into loud—very offkey—singing. "And with a little bit of red, green, and blue, I'll find my way back home to you. Oh babyyyyy," she bellowed into a paintbrush microphone. Her hips swayed side to side. "I'm coming back home to you."

Ellie covered her mouth to stifle a laugh. In

all of her twelve years, she had rarely seen her mother dance and sing like that. Penny stood at the top of the stairs with her mouth hanging open.

Mrs. Spark belted out another chorus before turning to the stairs with a hip pop, booty shake, and spin.

"Penny!" Mrs. Spark cried, freezing on the spot. Her face flushed red as she took off her headphones. "How long have you been there?"

Penny's white fangs shone as she let out a belly laugh. "Mom, I didn't know you could dance!" Her dress swished as she imitated the booty shake.

Mrs. Spark laughed. "What can I say? I'm full of surprises." She turned back to the dresser. "Did you need something?"

"Have you seen Ellie?" Penny asked.

Mrs. Spark tucked away her makeshift microphone. "No, sorry." She reached down and lifted the easel off the floor. "Whoops, must have knocked this over." She pushed the closet door shut as she walked back to the stairs. As the crack of light disappeared, Ellie and the

closet clutter were swallowed by darkness. The door sealed with a *click*.

"Maybe check downstairs," suggested Mrs. Spark.

The two sets of footsteps creaked against the stairs, but Ellie could barely hear them over her heart hammering. Not wanting to lose the game, she waited until they were gone to try to push the door open. But it wouldn't move. She realized that click had been the latch—she was trapped. Her breathing became fast and heavy as panic flooded her body.

"Mom! Mom!" she yelled. "You locked me in!" But there was no answer. The darkness surrounding her was like a snake coiling around Ellie's body. Every second she spent in the pitch-black closet, the tighter the grip felt, and the harder it was to breathe.

Chapter 2
The Unknown Caller

Tears flowed down Ellie's face as she gasped for air in the darkness. She banged on the closet door with her fists.

"Help!" she sobbed. "Get me out of here!" The tightness across her chest made every breath fast, loud, and shallow. She stopped to listen for footsteps over her breathing, but the only sound was the wind whistling through the window across the room.

"HELP!" she yelled once more. "I'm stuck. It's dark, and I can't breathe." Sweat trickled down her forehead as the closet suddenly felt like a scorching hot oven. A few moments later, small creaks and cracks came from the stairs. "I'm in the closet!" Ellie cried. "Open the door!"

"Ha! Found you! I win!" Penny boasted. "I

get your blood pudding for a whole week!"
The sound of food crunching filled Ellie's ears.

"Yes, you win. Now open the door. It's dark
in here, and I can't breathe."

"I think you're just being a Scaredy Bat and
pancaking," Penny said. "My friend Libby's
mom gets pancake attacks sometimes."

Ellie slammed her fist on the closet door re-
peatedly. "It's a *panic* attack, not a *pancake* attack. And I don't care what it is. I just want out
of here. It's small, dark, and a million degrees.

Mom! MOM!" she shouted.

The sound of food crunching once again echoed through the room. "She can't hear you," Penny said with a mouthful. "She has her headphones on."

"Penny. Let. Me. Out!" Ellie said through gritted teeth.

"If I let you out, what do I get?" Penny asked.

"You win and get my blood pudding all next week," Ellie said. "What more do you want?"

"Duh!" Penny exclaimed. "But I want to be let in your room anytime I want for a month."

"Fine! Just open the door." With a click, Penny unlatched the closet. Ellie burst out, taking in loud gasps of stale attic air.

Penny crunched down on the last of her carrot. "Wow, a whole month in your room! You should pancake more often." Ellie lunged toward her sister and chased her around the attic.

"I'm going to make *you* into a pancake," Ellie yelled. They wove around the easel before they scurried down the creaky stairs, all the way to the kitchen.

"Mom! MOM!" Penny cried. "Ellie is chasing me." They slid across the freshly cleaned floors with their sock feet. The smell of lemony cleaner lingered in the air.

Mrs. Spark was holding the phone to her ear. "Shh, I can't hear," she whispered.

"Is it Grandma?" Ellie whispered. "She is supposed to call me back about my necklace." Ellie clutched the purple dragon pendant hanging around her neck.

Mrs. Spark hushed Ellie. "I understand. That is quite the problem," she said to the unknown caller.

Ellie's mind wandered back to her last mystery at the amusement park. A gnome had told her that her necklace was special. Ever since then, she had been trying to learn more about it but couldn't find anything.

"Of course, Ellie is right here," Mrs. Spark said. "If she is interested, she can take her bike there later today." She handed Ellie the phone. "It's for you."

Ellie put it to her ear. "Hello?"

"Hello there, Miss Ellie!" said a chipper male voice. "How are you on this fine day?"

"Good," Ellie answered.

"Excellent," said the caller. "Then I'll cut right to the chase. My name is Henry Beagon from the Brookside Vampire Artifact Museum. And I'm calling because we have a mystery on our hands."

Ellie gasped as her heart fluttered with excitement. "A mystery!?"

"Yes, ma'am, a mystery. And I know that you are the absolute best detective in town, so I had to call you right away. I've already talked to your mother, and she said it would be okay if you and your detective team came down here to help out. That is, of course, if you don't already have plans today."

"No, sir, no plans!" Ellie said, dancing on the spot.

"Perfect! How about we meet at the museum, oh, let's say in an hour, around 3:00? Does that work for your schedule, Detective Ellie?"

"Yes!" Ellie said. "I just need to call my

friends to make sure they can come. I will see you at 3:00, Mr. Beagon."

"Looking forward to it." The phone call ended with a click.

"Mom! Someone called ME about a mystery!" Ellie squealed.

Mrs. Spark gave a big, fangy smile. "I heard! Congratulations, Detective Ellie."

"Can I go? Please, please, please!" Penny begged.

"Sorry, Mr. Beagon only asked for me and my detective team." Ellie's face was starting to hurt from smiling so hard. "I have to call Jessica, Fez, and Tink ASAP."

"But I want to go, too!" Penny complained, sticking out her bottom lip.

"You can help me pick an outfit for the art show tonight. It's at the museum, so we can meet Ellie there. I can't wait for you both to see my finished painting on display. Plus, I'll have a special surprise for you girls there." Mrs. Spark's smile faded. "That is, if they don't cancel the exhibit."

"Cancel it! Why would they do that?" Ellie

asked.

Mrs. Spark sighed. "Mr. Beagon said they might cancel if they can't solve the mystery. I will have done all that painting for nothing."

Ellie gave her mom a big hug. "It's okay; Detective Ellie is on the case!"

Mrs. Spark squeezed her daughter. "Just remember that you're still my little girl. It's okay if you don't solve *all* the mysteries. There will be plenty that need solving when you're older, but you're only a kid once."

"I know," Ellie said as she dialed the phone. "But I need lots of practice, because I want to be the best detective ever!" Before Mrs. Spark could reply, Ellie was already on her first call. "Hi, Mr. Fitzgerald. Can I talk to Fez, please?"

A few minutes later, Ellie let out a squeal of excitement as she hung up from her last call— all three of her detective friends were free. She dreamed about what the mystery could be as she packed her coat pockets with her notepad, magnifying glass, and fingerprinting kit. Was it some mysterious beast terrorizing the museum? Was there a magical spell that had to be

lifted? Ellie hoped it wasn't something like Mr. Beagon misplacing his glasses. Although, she would still be happy to help.

Any mystery was a good mystery. And there was only one way to discover what this one was all about.

Chapter 3

Vampire Artifact Museum

The chilly autumn air was crisp and energizing against Ellie's skin. It was extra refreshing when she peddled her bike up the steep hill to the museum. Halfway up, her legs burned like a million fire ants had stung her all at once. She stopped for a quick break, and to her delight, she was right beside the flyer she'd hung last week. The paper stapled to the wood pole read:

Best Detectives in Brookside. If you have a mystery, we can solve it. Call us today!

Front and center was a silhouette of the detective squad—Ellie, Jessica, Tink, and Fez. Ellie's purple dragon necklace was still colorful

and bright, though. Jessica had said "it will make the poster pop!" However, it was no longer the only color popping—along the bottom was a note scribbled in red marker.

Best detectives? They're just LITTLE KIDS!

Ellie's shoulders slumped. She remembered someone calling her last week about a lost cat. When they'd found out she was a kid, they said their cat "just walked in the door" and hung up. She tore down the flyer, crumpled it, and shoved it in her pocket. She was so tired of people not taking her seriously because of her age.

Not long after she started to peddle again, the museum's tree sculpture peeked over the hill's crest. The cement branches sprawled out from the trunk like spider legs. Each limb was enchanted to bear real fruit. Bright red apples, yellow bananas, and purple lemons called Violems created a rainbow against the gray cement.

Ellie parked her bike beside the gnome sculptures dancing around the tree base. The anger flowing through her melted as her hand

wandered to the cool metal on her necklace. One of the dancing gnomes with an apron and moustache looked exactly like the one she'd met at Mega Adventureland.

His words had been replaying in her head ever since: "That's a very special necklace. So rare. I've never seen one in real life." However, he never got a chance to tell Ellie why.

"Concentrate," she whispered to herself. "There will be time to figure out the necklace later." She turned away from the sculpture toward the museum. The red brick of the single-story building was warm and inviting against the dreary autumn sky. The long house with a flat roof and border of hedges was once a Vampire Inn—a secret place that hid traveling vampires from hunters. Once it outlived its purpose, the owner sold it to a museum developer before she left to look for her lost son.

Too excited to wait for the others, Ellie stepped around a massive mud puddle and climbed the stone steps. She ran her hand over the carvings of the fire-breathing dragons battling water demons on the double doors. The

breath of fire intertwined with the blasts of water wrapped around the cool brass door handles. She grabbed the knob and tugged. The door opened without a sound.

A comforting warmth washed over her chilly skin as she stepped inside. The smell of the entrance was lemony fresh, with a hint of flowers—just as she remembered. She couldn't count how many school field trips had been spent here over the years. Although, it got a little boring with very few new artifacts coming into the small museum. Ellie's mother said that was why they'd decided to explore other exhibits, like modern art.

An older man with a black suit and gray slicked-back hair walked toward Ellie. His shoes were almost as shiny as the black marble floors that tapped under his feet.

"You must be Detective Ellie," he said. "So pleased that you could come on such short notice." He gave her a small bow.

Ellie gave him a big, fangy grin. "That's me! And you must be Mr. Beagon."

"Right you are. But please, call me Henry." He tucked his clipboard under his arm and straightened his bowtie. "I was actually one of your grandfather's good friends."

"You were?" Ellie said, her mouth gaping slightly. Ever since her grandfather had passed away a couple years ago, she rarely heard anyone talk about him.

Henry gave a small smile. "I knew Leo for over forty years. I also know your grandmother quite well." He pointed to her necklace. "I recognized your necklace on your detective flyer right away. I remember your grandmother finding it on her Terrascope travels like it was yesterday."

Ellie gasped. "Can you tell me more about the necklace?"

Henry shook his head. "Afraid I don't know much more. I do believe there is some information on it in our Archive Room. But the problem is, I can't find the key. I think whoever took the artwork also stole the key to the archives. They both went missing today."

Ellie pulled her detective notebook from her pocket. "I'm guessing I'm here because of the missing art?" she said.

Henry nodded. "Right you are, Detective Ellie. Now, we should get to work. Follow me to the scene of the crime." Ellie tried to put on a serious face as they stepped into room 1B off to the left. But she couldn't stop smiling. Henry was treating her like a real detective.

An oversized chandelier with glimmering green and blue crystals hung in the middle of the ocean-blue room. She followed Henry as he wove between the round tables draped

with orange tablecloths. Each one was set with white plates and blue napkins centered around a vase of velvety black roses. There wasn't a wrinkle or a speck of dust in sight.

Henry arrived at a tarnished silver frame hanging on the wall. It was woven from carvings of branches and snakes. And whatever picture it had once held was ripped out. Pieces of the torn paper inside the frame gently flapped in the breeze from a nearby vent.

"This old painting was going to be the showpiece for the exhibit tonight, but someone tore it out," Henry explained. "We don't want to put any more art in danger, so we are thinking about canceling tonight's event."

Ellie bit her lip. She wanted to tell him he couldn't do that—her mom worked too hard. But she reminded herself that grownup detectives don't let their feelings interfere with a case. Instead, she tried logic.

"But why would the thief come back to steal more art?" Ellie asked "Wouldn't they just take it all the first time?"

"Perhaps," Henry answered. "But our

newest exhibit wasn't set up yet. It has a mix of art, including some from very important artists. We just got a shipment with some very valuable pieces today at 2:00."

"When did you notice the art was missing?" Ellie asked as she squinted at the frame.

Henry scratched his stubbly chin. "It disappeared sometime between 11:00 this morning and 2:00 while I was golfing. I noticed it was gone when I got back at 2:05 and called you right away." He groaned. "These events are always so stressful. I wish I didn't have to do them, but fewer and fewer people are visiting the museum since we get so few new artifacts. I really wish vampire families would see the value of putting special pieces on display instead of hoarding them." Ellie nodded and pulled her mom's makeup brush from her coat pocket. "What are you doing?" Henry asked with wide eyes.

Ellie dipped the brush in a small container filled with face powder. "I'm going to dust for fingerprints," she answered. She stepped toward the frame.

"Wait!" Henry cried. "You cannot touch that frame. Even without the art, it is a very valuable artifact." Ellie's face flushed hot with embarrassment.

"Sorry," she mumbled. Ellie tucked the brush in her pocket. She stood up straight as she realized something important. "I don't think someone did this for the art or the art's value," she observed.

"Why do you say that?" Henry asked.

"Because they ripped the painting and left the valuable frame behind," Ellie answered.

Henry grinned. "I knew I picked the right detective for the case. Great observation." He lowered his voice. "I thought of that too, but why else would they do such a thing?"

Ellie pulled out her notebook. "Maybe they wanted to ruin the exhibit tonight."

"Hmm, I think you're on to something," Henry said. He lowered his voice to a whisper. "Our curator, Clara Burg, wanted to submit a piece to the art show. But we have a strict rule about museum employees not participating in exhibits. We just can't risk looking like we have

favoritism. Anyway, today is her last day before retiring, so she asked if we could move the exhibit. That way, she could submit a painting. But unfortunately, the date was already set. She didn't seem very happy."

Ellie scribbled in her notepad.

Suspects

1. Henry Beagon — Hates events. Sabotage?
2. Clara Burg — Wanted art exhibit moved

Clues

1. Ripped painting

"So you think Clara ruined the painting to postpone the event?" Ellie asked.

Henry straightened his bowtie. "It is a possibility. Oh, but sweet Clara. It is so hard to imagine her doing such a thing. She has been with the museum longer than I have. I don't know. What do you think? You're the detective!"

Before Ellie could answer, the sound of laughter interrupted.

"Ellie? Ellie!?" came a loud whisper from the front door. "Sorry we're late."

Chapter 4

Best Detectives in Brookside

J essica, Fez, and Tink stepped into Room 1B, the dining room.

"There you are!" Jessica said. She took off her hood, shaking out her red curls. "Brr, it sure is chilly out there," she said.

Tink wiped his glasses off on his shirt. "It is actually unseasonably warm today. Although, I still think it is too cold for a slushie." Fez slurped on the swirly straw sticking out of a cup so big that it took two hands to hold.

"No way, it's never too cold for slushies," he said. He licked his lips with his blue tongue. "Especially sour raspberry!"

Henry cleared his throat as his eyes darted to the mud dripping off the trio's shoes. "I am

sorry, the museum is closed today to prepare for the gallery opening tonight," he said. "We would be happy to have you another time. Perhaps when you are a little less muddy." Jessica, Tink, and Fez followed Henry's gaze to the mud trail they'd made.

"Oops, sorry, "Jessica said. "But we're not here for a tour—we're here to solve the mystery."

Henry turned to Ellie. "These are your… associates, Detective Ellie?"

Ellie's mouth felt glued shut as her friends' muddy shoes dripped all over the previously spotless floors. Her face burned as she gave a small nod.

Henry groaned. "Very well, then." He snapped his fingers at Tink, who had pulled a towel from his backpack to mop up the mess. "No need for that." He lifted his boney wrist and spoke into a gold bracelet. "Carter, mud cleanup in Room 1B, ASAP."

"Got it," said a voice from the sparkling jewelry piece.

"Woah, that is awesome!" Tink said. "It's

so small and discreet. I didn't know they sold anything that tiny. Do you mind if I see it up close?" he asked.

Henry tucked the bracelet under his sleeve. "Maybe after we—"

Jessica gasped. "Are these Bat Breath Roses?" She ran a thumb over one of the black rose's velvety petals. She put her nose to one. "Wow, they really do smell like sweet cherries."

The loud slurping coming from Fez's straw stopped. "No way! That's so cool." He rushed to take a sniff, putting his drink on the tablecloth.

"No!" Henry squealed, rushing over. "These are super rare and were extremely hard to get for tonight's event." He scooped up the drink, but it was already too late—there was a water ring where the cup had sat.

"Sorry," Fez said with a blue grin, taking back his drink.

Henry whirled around to Ellie. "I am sorry, Miss Spark. Are you sure you and your... friends are up to this task?" He smoothed out the tablecloth. "I am on a ticking clock, and

I need the best detectives to solve this case."
He looked at Fez, who resumed slurping the
slushie. "You advertised yourselves as the
best—not sticky little sleuths who are going to
touch everything."

"No!" Ellie exclaimed. "We can do this." Jessica stood up a little straighter, smoothing out
her purple dress. "What do we know so far?"
she asked in a serious voice. Henry repeated
what he'd told Ellie and how they didn't think
the painting had been stolen for its value or the
artwork itself. Tink stepped closer to the painting as he listened. A distant crash and scream
pierced the air.

BEEP! BEEP! BEEP!

An alarm blared, and Fez jumped, spilling
his slushie on the floor.

POOF! Ellie turned into a bat and flapped
up into the chandelier.

Chapter 5

The Easiest Case Yet

Ellie, Jessica, Fez, Tink, and Henry followed the loud alarm to room 3B. They leapt over the mop and bucket in the doorway and into the flashing lights that bathed the art-filled room in an angry red glow. An eighteen-year-old boy with an uneven bowl cut stood in the middle of the chaos. Tucked under his arm was a soccer-ball-sized object. Beside him, an old woman cringed while cupping her ears.

"Henry! Turn this doggone alarm off!" she yelled. "You're going to make me deafer than I already am." Henry ran out of the room, and the wailing alarm and flashing lights stopped within a few seconds. The woman let out a sigh of relief. "Much better." The oversized gems on her rings sparkled as her shaky hands smoothed her dark braids pulled into a bun. Then she picked her tablet off the floor.

"Ah-ha! I think we caught our art thieves!" Fez said. "This was the easiest case yet." The woman and boy exchanged a confused look before bursting into laughter.

"We aren't art thieves—we work here," said the boy. "This is Clara, our art curator. And I'm Henry's grandson, Carter."

"I've worked here since before you youngins were born," Clara added. "If I wanted to steal art, I wouldn't have waited until my last day." She pointed to the ball under Carter's arm. "That head sculpture just came to life as I was hanging the work for tonight's show. One minute it was sittin' on that column all still, then BAM! It jumps off like it was some sort of bouncing bunny."

"Did you see this?" Ellie asked Carter.

"No," Carter answered. "I was grabbing a mop and bucket, but I raced in as soon as I heard the alarm. The alarm is pressure sensitive, so it goes off if anything is removed from the column. That means it would go off if this

guy accidentally got knocked down." Carter held out the sculpted marble head. A deep crack snaked between the eyes and down the nose. A yellow layer of crust sat in the left eye socket.

"*JUMPED* off the column," Clara corrected. "I know I can be clumsy, but this wasn't one of those times. If Henry wasn't so cheap and fixed the camera in this room, I could prove it!" She gave the head a good look, her lips drawing into a hard line. "Oh my, it is

completely ruined!" Tears filled her big brown eyes. "This was made by the great Spencer Eve over a thousand years ago. It's priceless." Clara fanned herself. "I think I need to sit down." Carter put the statue back on the podium and put his arm under a wobbly Clara. He led her to a bench under a painting of a duck filming a Ferris wheel filled with parrots.

Fez cringed at the statue's crusty eye socket. "Looks like the poor guy has an eye infection. I had one of those once, and it oozed yellow goop."

"Ew, Fez, TMI," Jessica said, her face turning slightly green. "It just looks like some sort of glue. I've used similar stuff when putting gems on clothing."

"It is glue," Carter confirmed. "This head used to have a big ruby eye before it fell off the column."

Ellie circled the room. Three walls were lined with paintings, and the other had columns with sculpted heads. She weaved between the art pieces—a donkey with a witch hat, a clown wearing a jellyfish as hair, a dragon king with a

monocle and mustache.

"Where did the ruby eye go after the statue fell—I mean, jumped?" Ellie asked. "I don't see it anywhere."

"Your guess is as good as mine," Clara said. "As soon as it happened, the alarm went off, and you youngins came racing in." Clara's hands clenched into fists by her side. "Maybe that troublesome ghost stole it! Sam Thomlin is always floating around causing havoc. Ever since that Terrascope exhibit we did a few months ago." She shook her head. "Good for nothin' ghost."

"Good for nothing?" Fez said. "Ghosts are great. They're so cool. Did you know they can disappear and reappear in puffs of smoke?" Clara looked up at Fez with her mouth gaping open.

"Not the time," Tink said behind a fake cough. Fez shrugged.

"Is there a way to find Sam?" Ellie asked.

Carter snickered. "No way. Sam doesn't answer to anyone. He's always just doing his own thing. I envy him. Although, if I were a ghost,

I sure wouldn't stick around this boring place."

"Do you think Sam would also rip that painting?" Ellie asked.

Clara gasped as her hand fluttered to her heart. "Is that what happened!? That ghoul ripped the canvas painting in there? Henry wouldn't let me in to see for myself." She scoffed. "He said he didn't want to risk any evidence getting ruined."

Ellie flipped her notepad. "It's not a canvas painting, it's paper. It has bits of paper still flapping in the corners."

Clara pursed her lips. "You're wrong, girlie. I know that it was a canvas painting. I even have a photo here on my tablet." She put on the glasses hanging around her neck and peeked over them at the screen. Then, after a few seconds, she let out a loud grunt. "Carter, how do I work this thing again? I can't keep up with all this new hullabaloo."

Carter pulled up the photos on the tablet. The first was of a man with an eyebrow scar and scruffy beard in front of paintings. The next was him hanging on the chandelier in

room 1B.

"Oh no, he didn't!" Clara cried. Photo after photo, it was the same man taking selfies all around the museum. "He did! That pesky ghost filled my whole tablet with self photos! And he deleted the other ones I had." The handful of pictures looped as Clara furiously scrolled.

"Wait! Go back to the one of him beside the marble statue head." Ellie said. She looked at the statue and then at the photo's date—two days ago.

Ellie's mouth fell open. "The broken statue is a fake!"

Chapter 6
Don't Lick the Evidence

C arter, Jessica, Tink, Fez, and Clara stared at Ellie.

"What do you mean the broken statue is a fake?" Fez asked. He squinted at it on the column. "It looks pretty real to me. Wait! Is this some sort of vampire intuition thing?" he asked. Ellie giggled. Fez and Tink were always so curious about vampire life.

"No," Ellie said. "I don't think there is such a thing as 'vampire intuition.' Although, that would be cool! Look at this." She held up the tablet with the selfie of the marble statue and Sam the ghost. "This was taken two days ago. If this is a photo of the real sculpture, this broken one has the ruby eye glued on the wrong side."

Clara clutched her heart. "Oh, this is too much for me." She adjusted one of her sapphire rings as she stood. "I need a cuppa tea to calm down. I'll be in the staff room if you need me."

"This is a great find, Ellie," Jessica said. "But how do we know this one isn't real and the one in the photo is fake?"

Ellie bit her lip. "I don't know. I just know they aren't the same."

"Wait, I know!" Tink said. He tapped the gold plate on the wall. It read:

'Head of Loki' by Spencer Eve
Carved from marble with a genuine ruby eye.

"I get it!" Carter exclaimed. "We can test the marble to see if it's real. I doubt whoever switched the head sprung for real marble. They probably stole the original sculpture for the value. If I could just remember how we learned to test marble at Science Camp..."

"That's it!" Tink exclaimed. "That's where I recognize you from. It was hard to tell with your new haircut! I'm Tink."

"Oh!" Carter said. "I remember you!" He

pushed his heavy, uneven bangs off his forehead. But they instantly popped back into place. He peeked over Tink's shoulder at the door to make sure Clara was gone. "Clara is planning on doing hair after she retires. So I volunteered to be her... test subject. But she's a little shaky with the scissors. Good thing she still gets paid after retirement thanks to the five years of vacation hours she saved."

"Not to interrupt, but can we get back to the investigation?" Ellie asked, tapping her foot impatiently. "How can we test the marble?"

"I must have something in here," Tink said. He plopped his backpack on the floor. Both boys knelt down and dug inside excitedly, like dogs looking for their favorite toy.

"Woah, it's like there are two Tinks," Fez whispered.

"I know," Jessica said. "Super freaky."

Ellie smirked. "Hopefully this means whatever they're about to do will go twice as fast."

"Ah-ha!" Tink exclaimed. He held up a small bottle of vinegar. "This will do the trick." He put a few drops on the statue head

and watched closely. "If it is real marble, it will bubble." They observed the drops for over a minute, but they were still.

"No bubbles," Tink concluded. "I don't think it's real."

Carter pulled a fork from the backpack. "Just to double-check your hypothesis, let's try to scratch it." He ran the prong across the sculpture's forehead. "Exactly as I thought, it doesn't scratch easily."

"That means it isn't real marble. Right?"

Fez asked.

"Bingo," said Carter.

"Does that mean that ruby on the floor over there is fake too?" Fez asked. He pointed to a red stone jammed in the heating grate.

"You found it!" Ellie cheered. She plucked up the hot, sticky gem and held it to the light.

"Every side is super scratched. That means it's real. Right?" Ellie said.

Carter shook his head. "Nope. Rubies are the opposite of marble—real ones don't scratch easily." Fez began loudly smelling the air. He sniffed all the way to Ellie's hand, grabbed the gem, and gave it a lick.

"Fez, don't lick the evidence!" Jessica exclaimed.

"I knew I smelled strawberry!" Fez said. "This is just candy."

"I guess that is one very unique way of figuring out what it is," Carter said. Everyone laughed.

"This is a great clue!" Ellie exclaimed.

"And a delicious one," Fez said, giving the fake eye one last sniff before handing it to Ellie.

Ellie held the sticky treat in her hand. "Now we just have to figure out what this has in common with the stolen painting. Let's get to work!"

Chapter 7
Emergency!

After looking over the ghost selfie and the fake statue head once more, Ellie jotted down her new clues and suspects.

Suspects

1. Henry Beagon – Hates events. Sabotage?
2. Clara Burg – Wanted art exhibit moved
3. Sam Thomlin's ghost – Stole real head to cause mischief?

Clues

1. Ripped painting
2. Fake marble head

Jessica peeked over Ellie's shoulder. "Why would someone ruin one piece of art and switch the other?" she asked.

"That's what I'm trying to figure out," Ellie answered. "Unless… Do you remember how Clara insisted that the other painting was canvas?" Jessica nodded. "Maybe that ripped painting wasn't real. What if someone is stealing the artifacts and breaking fake ones, so no one goes looking for the originals?"

Jessica stared at her best friend. "Ellie, that's genius! You're getting really good at this detective stuff."

"Or maybe they didn't plan on the statue breaking," Tink said. "After all, if the statue didn't break, maybe no one would have figured out it was fake."

"We would have figured it out in our weekly scan," Carter said. He looked up at the detective team, who were giving him blank stares. "Whoops, you're not supposed to know about that," he whispered.

"Why? What's a weekly scan?" Jessica asked.

Carter shushed her. "Keep your voice down.

I'll tell you, but you didn't hear it from me. All artifacts that came into the museum when it first opened were embedded with a rice-sized chip. These chips inhibit any magic from accidentally activating but are also supposed to allow us to track them if they're ever stolen."

Tink's mouth fell open. "You altered ancient artifacts!? But can't that ruin them?"

"Keep your voice down," Carter whispered. "That's how many people felt, so the program got scrapped and no tracking was ever added. It wasn't worth trying to remove the chips from objects that already had them, and certain metal scanning wands can detect them. My grandfather is overly paranoid and insists we scan all items with a chip weekly to make sure they're the real deal."

"Can't someone just put a chip in a fake item?" Tink asked.

"No," Carter answered. "The chips were made of a rare metal that is nearly impossible to find now."

"Does that ripped painting have a chip?" Ellie asked.

"Nope," Carter answered.

"Then we need to test it another way. C'mon, guys!" Ellie said to the group of boys. "We might need more of your science-y stuff."

Carter started to follow but quickly paused. "I would love to—this is the most exciting thing to ever happen in this boring place. But I need to stay here and clean up this mess. My grandfather will be mad if I don't." He gave a weak smile. "Good luck." Tink scanned the pieces of broken statue on the ground.

"Is it alright if I stay and help?" he asked Ellie. "I just want to catch up quickly, then I'll be back on the case."

Ellie groaned. "Tink, we're supposed to be investigating. This isn't very professional."

"It will only be a few minutes," Tink said. "I'm sure I won't miss much." Before Ellie could respond, Tink was already bent down, picking up chunks of stone. Annoyance zipped through her like a lightning bolt. And a faint squeaking off in the distance wasn't helping her irritation.

Fez put a hand on Ellie's back. "It's okay. We

can start without him. Let's go."

The trio ran down the hall. Loud voices boomed from behind a door marked 'Staff Only.' Jessica and Fez kept going, but Ellie paused.

"I know you've never picked up a paintbrush in your life. But these artists worked real hard on their pieces," Clara shouted inside. "If someone is hurting the art, you need to cancel the event. That missing statue head is a priceless vampire artifact, Henry. Priceless! Maybe you don't appreciate that because you're a

human, but it is a piece of our history. It's from a time when vampires were so busy running that they barely had time to make art. It was a symbol of hope for the future of my kind. It's a huge loss to the Brookside community."

"I'm just as devastated as you," Henry said. "I think you forget I've worked my whole life collecting vampire artifacts. I am not taking this lightly. But it is too late to cancel. Let's give the vampire girl a chance."

Clara sighed. "She's a mighty smart kid, but Charles, she's just that. She's just a kid." Ellie's stomach sank, and tears filled her eyes.

"For the millionth time, I don't like to be called Charles," Henry huffed.

"And I don't like to be disturbed during tea. So shoo," Clara said. "But think about what I said. *Henry*." With the sound of footsteps approaching the door, Ellie dove behind a nearby suit of armor. The words "she's just a kid" echoed in her head as Henry stomped past. With each repetition, her heart ripped apart further. She wiped the tears dripping down her face and whipped open her notebook. Beside

Clara's name she wrote *#1 Suspect!*

Jessica ran out of room 1B, her shoes screeching on the polished tile.

"Ellie! Emergency! Emergency!" she shouted. "The frame is gone!"

Chapter 8
Déjà Vu

Ellie rushed into room 1B with Jessica. Fez was staring at the blank wall where the ripped painting had hung before. He pulled a powdered donut hole out of his pocket and stuffed it in his mouth.

"Fez, you aren't supposed to be eating in here," Ellie hissed. "Real detectives don't snack on the case." Fez wiped his powder-covered fingers on his pants.

"Real detectives aren't doing it right then," he said with stuffed cheeks.

Squeak. Squeak. Squeak.

"You know detective work makes me snacky," he continued.

Ellie raised her finger to her lips. "Shh. Listen."

Squeak. Squeak. Squeak.

She tracked the faint sound to the wall. Just as soon as the trio pushed their ears against it, a distant crash boomed in the distance.

BEEP! BEEP! BEEP! The alarm went off.

"Woah, déjà vu!" Jessica yelled over the siren. Before they could leave the room to investigate, Tink raced in.

"The statue broke because it has a flip plate wired underneath!" he yelled. "Carter and I saw it. The top of the podium tipped, the statue head went flying, and the alarm started." The alarm turned off, and Tink took a deep breath. "Wait, where did that painting go?" he asked. They explained the missing painting and the squeaking sound.

Henry barged into the room. "What is happening?" he demanded. He gasped at the sight of Fez eating donuts. He pinched the bridge of his nose and squeezed his eyes shut. "I know that I did NOT just see you eating a powdered donut hole in my event room."

Fez froze, then shook his head. He went to shove the donut back in his pocket but dropped

it on the floor. A puff of white dust revealed
a red laser in front of where the painting used
to hang. Henry opened his eyes just as the dust
settled.

"Noooo," he squealed, looking at the pow-
dery mess. "This room was pristine. Perfect. A
work of art before you came in. Wait, where is
the painting frame!?"

Ellie gulped. "We just noticed it was
missing."

Henry puffed out his cheeks and exhaled

sharply. "I can't, I just can't. We will close the art room for tonight's event. People will enjoy the food and music." He plucked a black flower, put it to his nose, and inhaled deeply. "And these beauties."

Clara stood at the door. "Hallelujah! Now you're thinking," she said.

"But we just found a new clue!" Ellie exclaimed. "And some of those artists have been looking forward to having their art displayed!" Her heart ached thinking how sad her mother would be.

"I. Don't. Care!" Henry screamed. "Nothing is worth this—this mess." He lifted his small gold bracelet to his mouth. "Carter, print out new schedules for tonight. Remove the art room opening."

Carter groaned. "You sure you don't want to just close the museum until we figure this out? Maybe today can also be my last day in this boring place."

"We are not discussing this now," Henry said. "Get moving."

"Hold on," Jessica said. "Don't get rid of

the old schedules. If we solve this case, *which we will*, then you can open the exhibit."

Henry pinched the bridge of his nose. "Fine."

"I like this girl!" Clara clucked from the doorway. "She's fiery, just like her red locks. This is the first time I've seen Henry agree to someone else's idea in a long time. He's an old stubborn mule!" She took a shaky sip of tea.

"But I heard you say you also want to cancel!" Ellie blurted out. "Which would make sense, since you can participate if they move the show."

Clara waved her hand dismissively. "I wanted to cancel before we had a way to protect the art. I think this is a great plan. And even if we reschedule, the art is already picked, so this wouldn't be my show." She gave her bottom a shake. "At this point, I'm just ready to get my party on after my last day of work."

Ellie couldn't help but smirk at the woman's sunny attitude. She pulled out her notepad and scratched Clara's name off her suspect list. If she still couldn't take part in a postponed art show, she had no motive to get it canceled. However, the case did have a new suspect.

Suspects

1. Henry Beagon — Hates events. Sabotage?
2. ~~Clara Burg — Wanted art exhibit moved #1 SUSPECT!~~
3. Sam Thomlin's ghost — Stole real head to cause mischief?
4. Carter Beagon — Wants museum shut down because it's boring

Clues

1. Ripped painting (Missing)
2. Fake marble head (on remote controlled flip plate)

"I have an event security team and caterers to let in," Henry said as he made his way to the door. "You have until 5:00 to figure this out. And please, no more messes." The clock

on the wall read 4:00, giving them an hour.

Clara left too, but not before asking Fez for a powdered donut hole. He happily gave her one. As she dusted her hands, the red laser once again appeared.

"I think that may be a tripwire," Tink said once they were alone again. "You guys said you were by the wall when the alarm went off the second time. I was standing by the wall the first time. And if the laser is connected to the statue flip plate, that explains it."

"But what is the point?" Ellie asked.

"Maybe to lure us out of the room," Fez said. "So they could steal the frame."

"Why not just steal the frame when they ripped the painting?" Jessica asked.

"Maybe it was too heavy, so they needed more time? It is made of metal," Ellie answered.

"I hate to say this," Tink said. "But I am starting to suspect Carter. He is really good with technology and could have easily done this. Plus, he is always complaining about how boring it is here."

Ellie nodded. "Me too." Jessica lifted her shoe off the ground.

"Ick, what is so sticky on this floor!" she asked. She slipped off her shoe to look at the bottom. The white rubber had a layer of blue. The zingy smell of sour raspberry filled Ellie's nose.

"Oops," Fez said. "I think that is my slushie from earlier. The first alarm made me spill it." As the sun peeked out from a cloud through the window, it illuminated the floor. Sticky shoe prints smudged the tile. They trailed from where the painting had once hung to the room's door.

"I bet you those belong to the art thief!" Ellie said. She looked at the zig-zag pattern on Jessica's shoe sole. "These flat prints don't match Jessica's shoes. And no one else that we know of walked to the front of the room and back out." She followed the steps out into the hall, where they disappeared into the dark floor. Even with the shiny polish, the pattern made the steps impossible to follow.

"Looks like a dead end," Tink groaned.

"Hold on," Jessica said. "I have an idea. Fez, do you have any more pocket donuts?"

Chapter 9
Do Not Enter

Jessica sprinkled the donut's powdered sugar onto the black tile.

"What are you doing?" Ellie cried. "We aren't supposed to be making more messes."

Fez scowled. "Or wasting donut powder!"

"Hold on," Jessica said. She bent down and blew at the powder. The once-hidden footprint showed up like magic. "The powder sticks to the shoe prints," Jessica explained.

"That's genius!" Tink said. "You know, you could make a good scientist."

Jessica laughed. "Nah, that's your thing. Plus, I actually learned to do this by gluing glitter to clothes—ah-ah-achoo!" Jessica sneezed, and *POOF*, she turned into a rat.

Fez squealed with delight. "Sanalamia. I will

never ever, ever get sick of you transforming into a cute rat. I love that your vampire powers make it happen every time you sneeze." He popped her into the pocket with powdered sugar. "Whoops!" He pulled her back out and blew off her little paws. "Sorry," he whispered before putting her into the other pocket.

Fez took over the powder sprinkling, and they followed the prints all the way down the hall. Across from an office with a nameplate that read "Charles Henry Beagon" was a half-open metal door. In the middle hung a sign that said "Do Not Enter."

Ellie looked at her friends and gulped as they quietly slipped inside. The door closed with a soft click behind them.

Stepping over chunks of missing wood floor, they walked past a grand piano centered under a domed ceiling sparkling with stars. The surrounding walls were clad with dark wood bottom panels. On top were faded, painted murals. The footprints disappeared into a wall with vampires on one side under a starry night sky. On the other were humans in front of a

fiery sun. Lemon trees and bags of flour were scattered throughout the human side. On the vampire side were juicy red apples and plump grapes.

"Maybe the ghost walked through the mural," Tink said. "But then again, the frame can't just disappear through the wall."

"Woah, what is this mural?" Fez asked. He ran his finger over the gold line that divided the two species.

"It shows the war between vampires and humans," Ellie explained. "Before we started to live in harmony. This museum actually used to be a Vampire Inn, a place where vampires could hide from humans hunting them. On our last school field trip, they told us this room is where they used to throw parties to try to cheer up the families on the run. When the door of this room and the event room are shut, they are completely soundproof. There used to be live music and dancing almost every night."

Tink shook his head. "It's crazy to think some people still believe we should live separately. If that were true, we would never all be

friends."

Fez's shoulders slumped. "But you guys are my best friends. I don't know what I would do without you. There would be no mystery solving. And I wouldn't get to see my vampire friends transform into cute bats and rats." He took Jessica out of his pocket and hugged her against his face. She nibbled his nose.

"Aw, it's a love bite," Fez said. Jessica jumped out of his hands and scurried along the floor.

Tink giggled. "I think it might be more of a 'put me down' bite."

Ellie's eye wandered to a woman hugging a man in the middle of the painting. She couldn't see her face, but in her hand dangled a necklace.

"That's my purple dragon necklace!" Ellie cried. Tink squinted at the art and then at Ellie.

"You sure? That could be any purple pendant. It's kind of blurry."

"It's sort of small, but it looks just like mine!" Ellie said.

"Umm, guys," Fez said. They looked over

just in time to see Jessica squeeze her furry butt into a small crack in the wall.

"Jess, get back here!" Ellie said. "You don't know what is in there. There could be spiders, or termites, or—"

CRASH! A loud bang thundered in the wall.

"Jess? Jessica!" Ellie cried. "Are you okay?" The only sound in the room was the three friends' heavy breathing.

"Jessica?" Fez cried. He tugged at the wood panel, but it wouldn't budge. Tink pulled at a metal candlestick on the wall.

"If we can get this off, we can use it to rip open the hole to get to her!" he said.

"Achoo! I'm okay," came a quiet voice inside the wall. "The hole collapsed, so I can't get back out, though. And woah!" Jessica paused. "You aren't going to believe what is in here. Ah-ah-achoo!" She sneezed and turned back into a rat.

After fifteen minutes, Jessica was still trapped. They tried pushing on panels and searching for a button, key, or anything to get inside. They found a keyhole hidden in the

mural, but no key anywhere.

"We need to see if there is some other way to open the door," Tink said. "Maybe a backup in case the key is lost. Or, in our case, can't be found." Fez's stomach grumbled, and Tink shot him a look.

"Sorry, staring at all the apples and fruit on this mural is making me hungry."

"Wait, what do you think this carving in this tree means?" Ellie asked. "'Sing to the stars for the key. Start with apple, apple, grape, grape. Then two times something lemony.'"

"Achoo!" came a sneeze from the other side of the wall. Jessica sighed. "I'm never getting out of here, am I?"

Fez stood up straight. "I'll get you out." He tipped his head to the ceiling and started singing. "Apple, apple, grape, grape, something lemony, lemony. This is my song for the starrrrrs." With no better idea, all the friends joined in. After a few choruses of nothing happening, they looked for a new plan.

"Hold on, there are apples in this painting," Ellie said. She located a bunch and took out

her magnifying glass. "And there is some sort of music note written on this one."

Fez peered through the glass. "That's a G note." Next, they located a lemon with an E note and grapes with a D note. Ellie and Tink looked at each other and shrugged.

"I'm not very good at music," Tink said.

"Me neither," Ellie said. "I have no idea what this means." Fez pulled the bench out from the piano in the middle of the room and took a seat.

"I think I know!" he said. He hit the keys one by one—G, G, D, D, E, E. The tune to "Twinkle Twinkle Little Star" floated through the room. The stars on the ceiling grew brighter with each note.

Squeak. Squeak. Squeak.

The wall panel lifted with the final note, revealing the secret room with a soft blue glow.

Jessica ran out. "I had no idea you could play music!" she said. "That was so good."

"Thanks," Fez said with a smile. "The pigs on the farm used to like it when I played for them."

She laughed. "That story doesn't surprise me one bit. Now come on."

Chapter 10
Intruder Alert

Ellie, Jessica, Tink, and Fez crammed into the secret room. One of the security monitors mounted to the wall read 4:30, which meant they only had thirty minutes left to solve the mystery. The screens' light bathed the desk scattered with electronic parts in a blue glow. And in the corner were the frame and marble statue head.

"We did it!" Ellie said. "Whoever has access to this secret room is probably our thief." Tink picked up a screwdriver off the desk.

"I think we know who it is," he said.

"And who it isn't," Jessica said. "Look at this letter. It's from the Museum Board and says that if Henry doesn't bring in money from events this year, they will replace him."

69

Ellie pulled out her notepad. "If that's true, there is no way he would want to sabotage the event. He seems to care about this place a lot. He freaks out every time something gets a little dirty."

Suspects

1. ~~Henry Beagon — Hates events. Sabotage?~~
2. ~~Clara Burg — Wanted art exhibit moved #1 SUSPECT!~~
3. Sam Thomlin's ghost — Stole real head to cause mischief?
4. Carter Beagon — Wants museum shut down because it's boring

Clues

1. Ripped painting (Missing)
2. Fake marble head (on remote controlled flip plate)
3. Secret room with monitors and stolen artifacts

Fez peeled back the ripped paper in the frame. Underneath was a colorful field with a couple sitting on the edge.

"The real painting was underneath the whole time," he said. On one monitor, Carter mopped the sticky footprints off the floors. On another, Henry was locking up the archive room.

"Wait, can you rewind these security cameras to get proof?" Ellie asked. "This isn't looking good for Carter, but good detectives always need evidence." After looking around

the monitors, Tink shook his head. "These aren't the kind that record. They only have a live feed."

Squeak. Squeak. Squeak.

The gang whirled around to find the door closing. It fell closed with a thump just as the security monitors turned off. They were enveloped with darkness.

"What just happened?" Jessica asked.

"Hold on, I have a flashlight," Tink said. The sound of her friends' voices soothed Ellie. Being in the dark with them was always much easier than being alone. Although, she was edgier than usual. The hairs on the back of her neck stood up as her necklace slid upward.

"Got it!" Tink said, flicking on a flashlight. Ellie, Tink, Fez, and Jessica screamed. A man with a scar running across his eyebrow stood beside Ellie. He snagged the necklace and disappeared in a puff of smoke.

Jessica's breath heaved. "Did you see that?"

"Yes," Tink said. "We have to get out of here."

"But my necklace!" Ellie yelled. "The ghost

stole it!"

"Shh!" Jessica said. "You're being loud."

"It's a soundproof room—it's not like Carter can hear us," Ellie huffed.

"Either way, Tink is right," Jessica said. "Look for something to open that door." They ripped through the parts on the desk and crawled underneath but didn't find anything. After a minute of digging around, Fez spoke.

"Found it!" He pushed a red button by the door.

"Intruder alert, intruder alert," blared a voice over the speakers. A whiny alarm screeched through the room.

"I am so sick of alarms!" Jessica said, covering her ears.

"If Carter didn't know we were here before, he does now," Tink said.

Chapter 11
Millions of Messes

The four friends scurried around the cramped room, searching for something to open the door.

"Okay, plan B," Jessica said. She pointed to a vent on the wall. "We crawl out."

"What is that pesky alarm?!" bellowed Clara. It sounded like she was right outside the secret door. They quickly unscrewed the grate and climbed in. The metal shaft squeaked and groaned with each movement.

"This isn't our quietest escape," Jessica whispered. They made it around a corner before the vent cracked underneath them. They tried to crawl faster, but the end of the open shaft crashed through the ceiling. They slid down and fell onto bags full of flour. They coughed

and spluttered as puffs of the white powder blocked their view.

"Achoo!" Jessica sneezed and turned into a rat just as Henry appeared through the cloud of dust. His face was redder than the tomatoes on the metal table beside him. The caterers putting together trays stood with their mouths gaping.

"Get. Out!" Henry yelled. "You and your sticky drinks, powdered donuts, and millions of other messes are never to come to this museum again. You're fired!"

"But you don't understand," Ellie said. "Someone stole my necklace, and we think Carter—"

Henry shoved the group to the front door. "I don't care to hear your stories. I should have never trusted a silly little kid."

"Hey, that's not fair!" Fez shouted. "Ellie is—"

"Kicked out forever, as are the rest of you. Now goodbye," Henry snarled. He slammed the doors behind the trio on the front steps. Tears stung Ellie's eyes as she ran to the tree sculpture.

"Ellie, it's okay," Fez said.

"It is not!" Ellie cried. "I was finally getting taken seriously, and you guys had to ruin it. Fez and your drinks and food everywhere. And Tink, you were so busy with Carter that you were missing important parts of the mystery. It was so unprofessional."

"Woah, if I hadn't stayed back to help him, we may have never figured out the statue flipping thing," Tink said. "And Fez's snacks revealed important clues."

Ellie ignored him and scribbled in her detective notes.

Suspects

1. ~~Henry Beagon — Hates events. Sabotage?~~

2. ~~Clara Burg — Wanted art exhibit moved #1 SUSPECT!~~

3. Sam Thomlin's ghost — Stole real head to cause mischief? Stole my necklace!!!

4. Carter Beagon — Wants museum shut down because it's boring

Clues

1. Ripped painting (Missing)
2. Fake marble head (on remote controlled flip plate)
3. Secret room with monitors and stolen artifacts

Fez patted Ellie's head. "You should be happy. We figured out that Carter was behind

it. We solved the mystery."

Ellie moved away from the gesture. "No. Something feels off," she said. "Carter does all this so he doesn't have to work at the museum? How does that relate to the ghost that stole my necklace?"

"Maybe they're unrelated," Tink suggested. Fez snapped a picture of the museum with a black and silver camera.

Ellie shook her head. "My detective gut is telling me they're connected somehow."

Fez circled the tree. "Guys, we lost Jessica. I think she turned into a rat and is still inside!"

"Now we lost Jessica. Great!" Ellie said sarcastically. "What if she can't get out? Or what if one of us squished her falling out of the vent!" She ran back to the front door and gave it a tug, but it was locked. Next, she raced to the side of the brick building and tried to see through the windows. One by one, she scanned the rooms, but there was no Jessica. She squinted into an office with pasty green wallpaper, a portrait of a squirrel wearing a crown, and two desks. Suddenly, a rat scurried

over her foot.

"Jessica!" Ellie squealed. She scooped up the furry creature and hugged it. "I thought I lost you."

"Gee, must be nice not to be yelled at," Tink mumbled.

Fez kicked a cluster of crunchy leaves. "Right?" Ellie's stomach sank as she thought back to what she had said to them a couple minutes ago.

"I'm sorry I was mean," she said. "I hate that people just think I'm a little kid so I can't be a real detective. It was nice to be treated like a grownup for once. But here I am, acting like a kid blaming you guys."

Tink sighed. "I get it. Most people don't take me seriously when I'm doing science experiments either."

Fez scratched rat Jessica under the chin. "But guys, don't we have our whole lives to be taken seriously? I kind of just want to have fun and be a kid!"

Ellie smirked. "That's true. I'll try to remember that next time I'm frustrated." A tap came

from the inside of the office window, causing the three friends to jump. Jessica opened the window.

"Hurry up. I could only turn the window alarm off for a minute or two." Ellie wrinkled her nose as she held up the rat she was petting. She placed it in the grass, and it scurried away.

"Wait, we can still be friends!" Fez called after it.

"Shh!" Jessica said. "Get in so we can search for evidence to prove it was Carter. You can make friends with random rats later."

When they were all inside, Ellie threw her arms around Jessica. "I'm so happy you're okay."

"Of course I'm okay," Jessica said. "And I can't believe you thought I was that rat. I'm way cuter." They all laughed.

"Now let's find some evidence!" Tink said.

Chapter 12
C.B.

The four friends started their office search in the bigger desk's drawers. Pencils and pens were lined up in neat rows, and papers were perfectly stacked. The smaller desk was the opposite, with piles of messy papers, gum wrappers, and a moldy box of biscuits.

Ellie turned to the seashell clock on the wall. There were only fifteen minutes before people arrived at the art show. And she bet they wouldn't be allowed in the art room. The image of her sad mother floating through her head made her heart ache. She tugged at a filing cabinet, but it was locked. Next, she pulled out her detective notebook and scanned it for inspiration.

Suspects

1. ~~Henry Beagon — Hates events.~~ ~~Sabotage?~~

2. ~~Clara Burg — Wanted art exhibit moved #1 SUSPECT!~~

3. Sam Thomlin's ghost — Stole real head to cause mischief? Stole my necklace!!!

4. Carter Beagon — Wants museum shut down because it's boring

Clues

1. Ripped painting (Missing)
2. Fake marble head (on remote controlled flip plate)
3. Secret room with monitors and stolen artifacts

They flipped through books on the shelf looking for secret papers slipped inside or hidden passageways. When that didn't work, they searched through the trash. They dug through tissues, wrappers, and other odd and ends but didn't find anything useful.

As Fez bent down to tie his shoe, a donut slipped out of his pocket and rolled under the big desk. "Whoops," he whispered. He picked it up, gave it a blow, and popped it in his mouth. Jessica cringed and stuck out her tongue. "What? Five-second rule," he said.

Jessica giggled. "At least wipe the evidence away." She got down on her hands and knees and brushed the powder off the carpet. Just then, a shiny metal key taped to the bottom

of the desk caught her eye. "I think I found the filing cabinet key!" she exclaimed. With a click, the drawer rolled open.

"We need to find something that proves Carter did this. Or that he partnered with Sam Thomlin," Ellie said. "Look for something with Sam's name or Terrascope Travels."

Jessica thumbed through the files and paused halfway through.

"What about one with your name?" she asked Ellie. She pulled out a file labelled "E. Spark" and took out the contract inside. It was signed by the initials S.T and C.B. They read it over silently, and Fez clicked a picture with a camera.

Jessica blinked rapidly from the blinding flash. "Where did you get a camera?" she asked.

"It was in that secret room," Fez mumbled. "I accidentally took it. But it's so cool! It must be super old. Is it so wrong to steal from someone that steals?"

"Yes!" Ellie, Jessica, and Tink said in unison.

Fez groaned. "But what if it has some

evidence on it? Then can I keep it?"

Jessica grabbed the camera and turned it over in her hand. "It's an old camera with film, so it would have to be developed. We don't exactly have time or tools to do that right now. It's a good idea, but you still have to give it back."

Fez slumped as he grabbed the camera. "Fine."

Tink flipped to the next page of the contract. "Woah, this is proof," he said. "C.B. signed this contract with S.T. C.B must be Carter Beagon, and S.T is Sam Thomlin. It states that Carter will give Sam certain artifacts if Sam gets him... Ellie's necklace."

Ellie grasped her bare neck. "What!? Why would Carter want my necklace?"

The office door burst open. Carter stepped inside with his arms crossed. "You tell me."

Chapter 13
Proof

Carter shut the door behind him, and the mystery team backed away.

"I know my grandfather kicked you all out, so how did you get back in here?" No one answered. Carter ran his hands through his uneven mushroom cut. "Fine, then tell me what you think I did. You think I stole some necklace? I could hear you through the door." Ellie stepped forward onto the cushy area rug. Her hands shook as she planted them on her hips.

"That's exactly what we think," she said. The contract shook like a leaf in her hands as she picked it up. "And we—we have the proof. These are your initials."

Carter snatched the contract. "I didn't sign this. Someone else with the same initials must

have." Everyone was quiet as he read over the contract. Until soft chewing came from Fez popping donut holes in his mouth.

"How deep are your pockets?" Tink asked.

"Deep!" Fez said with a mouthful.

"You know those touched my little rat feet when you put me in your pocket, right?" Jessica asked.

Fez popped another in his mouth and shrugged. "Doesn't bother me."

Carter shushed them. "Wow, whoever did sign this contract is in a lot of trouble," he said.

"Why should we believe it wasn't you?" Jessica asked.

Carter scratched his head. "For one, I want nothing to do with necklaces or other old trinkets. I want to work on new stuff. The only reason I'm still here is because I love spending time with my grandpa. I don't know how to break it to him that I don't want to work in the museum. Truth is, I am taking an electronics internship this January." He placed the contract back on the desk. "You know, you think he would understand. He loves technology just

as much as I do. He's the one who taught me everything I know. He should be proud."

"So that secret room with the video monitors isn't yours?" Ellie asked.

"The what?" Carter laughed. "I can't even get my own office around here, let alone a secret room."

"I thought this was your office," Jessica said.

Carter shook his head. "Nope, Clara shares it with my grandfather."

After Carter showed Ellie a document of how he wrote his initials, she scratched his name off her suspect list. While his 'C' had a crooked swoop, the one on the contract was so symmetrical it looked like a computer could have typed it.

Clues

1. Ripped painting (Missing)
2. Fake marble head (on remote controlled flip plate)
3. Secret room with monitors and stolen artifacts

Suspects

1. ~~Henry Beagon — Hates events.~~
   ~~Sabotage?~~

2. ~~Clara Burg — Wanted art exhibit~~
   ~~moved #1 SUSPECT!~~

3. Sam Thomlin – Stole real head to
   cause mischief? Stole my necklace!!!

4. ~~Carter Beagon — Wants museum~~
   ~~shut down because it's boring~~

Ellie looked back at the name 'Clara Burg.' "Wait, Clara has the initials C.B."

"And she really likes jewelry," Jessica added. "She could have even stolen the statue head for the ruby."

"I think your best bet is going to talk to her," Carter said. "If she does have your necklace, she is heading out of town tomorrow. You need to catch her before it's too late."

"But aren't you going to tell on us for sneaking back inside?" Ellie asked.

"Yeah right," Carter said. "This is the most

interesting day at the museum ever. I want to see how this turns out. Follow me. I know where she is." Ellie stood still, unsure.

"Trust him," Tink whispered. With a deep breath, Ellie did just that. They followed Carter down the hall, and Ellie tried not to stare at how uneven his bowl cut was in the back. She couldn't imagine cutting hair would go well for Clara with such shaky hands. Her mind shot back to the contract's straight and clean initials, and her heart skipped a beat.

"I think we might be wrong about Clara—" she started. But the sight of Henry crossing the hall made them all scramble. Ellie stumbled into knight armor. Then, with a *thunk* and a crash of metal, her elbow smashed into a brick. The wall opened, swallowing her and the knight. She screamed as she slid down the slope into the damp, chilly basement. Then, just as quickly as the secret wall chute had opened, it closed.

Ellie was enveloped in darkness.

Chapter 14

Knight in Shining Armor

Ellie stood, shaking and alone in the pitch-black basement.

"Hello? Hello!" she yelled, but no one seemed to hear her. "Henry is behind this!" she called out. "You need to stop him before he gets away with the necklace. His real initials are C.B—Charles Beagon." She backed herself into a wall and slid down it. Pulling her knees to her chest, she rocked herself.

She sat there listening to her heart hammering mixed with dripping water. Slowly, she ran her hands over the cold brick strung with cobwebs. She clutched her throat as her breath hitched in the back. She couldn't see a thing. She clamored over the hunk of armor that fell with her, wishing a real knight would save her.

"It's just darkness. It's just darkness," she told herself. "Nothing to be afraid of. Or, as Penny would say, have a 'pancake' attack over." The thought of her silly sister brought a slight smirk to her face. She took a deep, shaky breath. "I've come this far solving this mystery; I am not going to let a little darkness stop me now. I can do this."

She felt her way to the next wall looking for a light switch. She ran her hands over rough wood shelves and cold, leaking water pipes but couldn't find what she was looking for.

After no luck, she decided to turn into a bat and use echolocation to get out.

POOF! She transformed and suspended herself in the air. She opened her mouth and made a series of popping and clicking sounds. Finally, she was able to find the chute she'd come down. But she also found something that sent a shiver through her body—someone was standing in the room with her.

POOF!

"Who's there! What do you want?" Ellie

cried at the mystery person.

"To give you back your necklace," said a deep voice. The light flicked on, revealing the empty, leaky basement. There were only a few dusty shelves and a pile of broken chairs.

"Don't be alarmed," Sam said, holding up his hands. From the left, the necklace dangled. "I can explain everything." Ellie marched up to him with a burst of bravery and snatched her pendant.

Sam gave a crooked smile. "Nice to see feistiness runs in your family."

"What is that supposed to mean?" Ellie asked while analyzing her necklace.

Sam shook his head. "A story for another time." He pulled another dragon pendant out of his pocket. "That is the real one. I just needed to borrow it to make a fake. I was hoping to give it back before you even knew, but being sneaky was never my strong suit."

Ellie squinted at the man with his bushy salt-and-pepper beard and kind green eyes. Something about him seemed familiar, but she couldn't put her finger on it.

"Why would you give Henry a fake?" Ellie asked. "Aren't you worried he will take back all the artifacts that you STOLE?" She wasn't sure where her bravery was coming from. But her whole body tingled with a fiery warmth. Sam sat down on a rickety wooden chair that looked like it would crumble any second.

"I worked my whole life finding artifacts and putting them back where they belong. I've always believed that artifacts are meant to

95

be used, especially vampire ones. They aren't meant for stuffy museums for people to gawk at."

Ellie eyed his perfectly flat teeth as he smiled. "But you aren't even a vampire," she said. "Why do you care?"

"You don't need to be something to care about it," Sam explained. "You have human friends, don't you? And you love them even though you're a vampire."

Ellie pulled the necklace back over her head, and her voice softened. "Yes. But why should I believe you about the necklace? How do I know these aren't both fake?" Sam stood up, reached into his pocket, and pulled out a photo.

"This should help. When you're ready, grab this and it will take you back upstairs," he said. "I'm afraid it will be a dark journey, but you can stop Henry. Just give me two minutes to give Henry the necklace and get out of here. Oh, and tell your friend Fez he can keep my old camera."

"Wait! You can't just leave me here!" Ellie

said.

"You can leave as soon as you grab that photo," he said. His eyes went glassy. "And please, tell your grandma that Sam says hello." Before Ellie could ask how he knew her grandmother, he disappeared in a puff of white smoke.

She rushed over to the photo on the chair. Her eyes trailed over the black and white ink that showed her grandmother laughing with a man. She couldn't be more than eighteen. Her hair was dark like Ellie's, and she wore the dragon necklace around her neck. Her fangs contrasted the man's flat teeth, and she appeared to be touching a scrape on his eyebrow. Taking a deep breath, Ellie picked up the photo. Suddenly, her body rocketed through the air as if it were zooming down an invisible waterslide. Unable to move any of her limbs, she sped through the blackness. A small speck of light grew bigger with every second until it swallowed her whole.

With a sputtering sound, she landed on the hall floor beside Jessica.

"Oh, sweet pudding! We were so worried!" Jessica said. She dove to the floor and gave Ellie the tightest hug. "Where did you go? How did you get back?" As Jessica released Ellie, she picked up the pendant. "And how did you get this back?" she asked.

"I'll explain later," Ellie said. "Where did the boys go?"

"To interrogate Clara," Jessica answered.

Ellie shook her head. "It isn't Clara. Her hands are too shaky to make initials that neat. We need to find Henry. AKA Charles Beagon. Let's go!"

Chapter 15

I Remember Everything

Ellie ran into the dining room just as Henry was giving a speech to the crowd of guests. "I want to thank you all for being here tonight. We weren't sure if we would be able to open the exhibit due to some thefts."

Gasps and whispers erupted from the crowd.

Henry adjusted his bowtie. "But don't worry, I solved the case."

"Yeah, you're the thief!" Ellie shouted.

Henry's eyes widened. "Security! This little girl has been banned from the museum for life. Please show her out." Ellie's mother stepped out of the crowd, her red dress sparkling under the chandelier's glow.

"Excuse me. You will not be kicking out my daughter," she exclaimed.

Henry pinched the bridge of his nose. "Fine, stay. Have some food and drinks. Just, please, don't interrupt."

"Kind of hard to do when you lured me here to steal my necklace. But guess what?" Ellie pointed to it. "I got it back." Henry's face turned a sickly white as he patted his pocket. "Whatever is in your pocket is fake," Ellie added.

Henry took a sip of wine and gave an awkward laugh. "Come on, why would I want a silly trinket? Is anyone actually going to believe this little girl?"

Ellie's grandmother stepped out of the crowd. "I sure am!"

"Grandma!" Ellie cheered. She lunged toward her grandma and hugged her.

"Hi, Pudding Pop," Grandma said before kissing Ellie on the head. She turned her focus back to Henry.

"Now, I know, Henry, that you didn't just call my granddaughter a liar." She stepped toward him, her short heels clicking loudly in the quiet room. "Surely not after chasing that

necklace for the last forty years. My whole career trying to get artifacts back to their rightful families, I had you nipping at my heels. 'This belongs in a museum,' you said. 'Vampires are going to die out and don't need these things,' you said."

Shocked faces in the crowd quickly turned red with anger. They advanced toward Henry, bumping Ellie left and right. Ellie untangled from the group just as the parents of her friend Ava Grinko slipped out the front door.

"She's exaggerating," Henry said, backing away. "I think old age is getting to you and you aren't remembering correctly."

"I remember everything," she snarled. "And I'm going to add what you did to my grandbaby to the list."

Henry wiped a bead of sweat off his forehead. "Fine! Do you want me to admit that I stole the real painting and statue and broke the fake one? Because I did." The crowd paused. "Unfortunately, Ellie and her pesky friends were better detectives than I expected. I thought 'Oh, she's just a kid, so I can get her

to think it's Clara who committed the crime.' I didn't want to have to pay that old bat five years of saved vacation days when she retires. And if she were caught stealing, I wouldn't have to!"

Clara stood at the back of the room with Tink, Fez, and Carter. "You always were cheap!" she yelled. "Unless it comes to the flowers for events. Those roses cost more than you pay me in a year!"

Henry rolled his eyes. "All I wanted was to finally get that necklace *and* get rid of Clara all in one swoop. But I guess it's true what they say—you can't have it all. I should have just gotten the necklace and reported those artifacts stolen for the insurance money."

Clara shook her head. "You always did make things more complicated than they needed to be." Bright car lights blinked through the window.

"Woah! What's that?!" Henry yelled. He bolted past the distracted crowd and out the front door.

Almost every guest raced after him, but he

was already hopping in a car by the time they got outside. The white SUV's tires screeched as it sped away. The flash of Fez's camera went off, leaving Ellie seeing white spots.

"Boy, if you are going to use that camera, you better figure out that flash," clucked Clara. Everyone laughed but Ellie.

"You okay?" Grandma asked.

Ellie sighed. "Yes, but I can't believe he got away."

Ellie's grandma gave her a squeeze. "Still a mystery well solved. Now, let's go home so I can tell you about your necklace."

Chapter 16
Sweet and Spicy

Ellie grabbed a tray of hot chocolate from her mother in the kitchen. The smell was sweet and comforting. And just a bit spicy thanks to a dash of red pepper.

"Are you sure you aren't sad about the art show?" Ellie asked for the tenth time.

"Stuff happens," Mrs. Spark said. "There will be other art shows. Better art shows. Plus, I missed your dad for this one. Maybe I will pick the next one for when he isn't working out of town."

Ellie grinned. "I like that idea." She brought the warm drink to her friends in the living room. Penny was already passed out, snoring on the couch, but Jessica, Tink, and Fez were all gathered around her grandmother. After

the warm drinks were handed out, Ellie sat down, and her grandmother started.

"I found the necklace on one of my digs, and I knew it was special as soon as I held it." Ellie clutched where her dragon pendant usually hung on her chest, but all she got was a fistful of air. She must have slipped it off when she took off her detective coat. "It wasn't long before I figured out it could grant wishes," Grandma continued.

Fez turned to Ellie. "You're like a genie!"

Grandma laughed. "Not quite. You see,

only Ellie gets to make the wish. Or whoever is wearing the necklace. She can't give the wish away. And she only gets to make a wish if the bravery meter is full."

"What's that?" Tink asked. He slurped his hot chocolate, which gave him a marshmallow mustache.

Grandma licked her thumb and cleaned his face before continuing. "You see, every time Ellie did something really brave, it would fill the meter, and she could then make a wish. It couldn't just be anything that takes courage though—it had to be a big thing. And every time she got scared, it would drain some of the wishing power."

Jessica leaned closer to the crackling fireplace. "How do you know when it's ready for a wish?"

"It glows," Grandma answered.

Fez gasped. "I saw it do that one time! Remember, at the Garlic Festival in the tent. Ellie dressed up as a clown even though she was afraid of them."

"I do remember," Tink said. "Freaky. What

wish did you get, Ellie?"

Ellie shrugged. "I don't remember wishing for anything… wait! But I do remember wishing for Jack to turn purple after our jellyfish mystery!"

Grandma laughed. "You're telling me you used your wishing power to turn some boy purple?"

"I think I also wished for our first mystery when the royal wedding got frozen. AND that there were enough tickets for all of us to go to Mega Adventureland after that movie set mystery." Ellie paused, then gasped. "I just remembered, I did wish for something after the Garlic Festival. I wished to meet Hailey Haddie!"

"Those sound better than turning a boy purple," Grandma said with a fangy smile. "Now, I have to get some shut-eye."

"Wait! I have so many more questions," Ellie said. "Why didn't you tell me about how special the necklace was before? Why did you give something so powerful to me in the first place?"

Grandma dug a tattered leather journal out of her giant purse. "I think this will answer some of your questions," she said. Ellie ran her fingers over the leafy vines burnt into the cover and faded gold initials, 'L.L.' "This journal belonged to your Grandpa Leo," Grandma explained. Ellie flipped through the tatty, yellow pages packed with drawings and writing.

Grandma kissed all the kids on the forehead before scooping Penny off the sofa. "Goodnight," she whispered before carrying Penny to bed.

After discussing what Ellie would wish for now that she knew about the necklace, the mystery team headed to the front door.

"You guys are the best!" Ellie said before they left. "I'm lucky to have friends as great as you."

"We're lucky to know a detective as great as you. And I suppose you're a pretty good friend," Jessica said with a wink. "See you tomorrow!"

Ellie couldn't stop yawning as she headed to her bedroom. As much as she wanted to read

the journal, her eyes were heavy and bleary. She figured she wouldn't get past the first page before falling asleep. As she bent down to slip it under her mattress, the photo that Sam had given her fell from her pocket and fluttered to the floor. Ellie poked it before picking it up— afraid it would transport her again. She could safely say she was done with museums for a while.

Once it seemed safe, she picked up the photo and went to the attic.

Creak. Crack. Creak.

"Grandma," Ellie whispered at the top of the loud stairs. Grandma sat on the end of a cot in the middle of the art studio.

"What can I do for you?" she asked.

Ellie held up a photo. "I met a man named Sam Thomlin today, and he asked that I say hi to you. I also think you may want this." She handed the old photo to her grandma.

"My, does this bring back memories," Grandma said with tears running down her cheeks. "He was my best friend when I was just a little older than you." She sighed. "That

feels like a lifetime ago now. Oh, my sweet Ellie, don't be in too much of a rush to grow up. It goes so fast." She clenched the photo to her chest.

"I won't," Ellie whispered. She cuddled beside her grandmother in the small cot. "Why have I never heard of Sam before?" she asked after a couple minutes. But the only answer she got were small snores.

As Ellie drifted to sleep, she thought about her friends and all their adventures.

Someday she would be an adult. And everyone would know to call Detective Ellie for their mysteries. She was excited for that day. But she decided she didn't want to rush it. For now, being a junior detective and even a Scaredy Bat was fine by her.

Hi!

Did you enjoy the mystery?

I know I did!

If you want to join the team as we solve more mysteries, then **leave a review**!

Otherwise, we won't know if you're up for the next mystery. And when we go to solve it, you may never get to hear about it!

You can leave a review wherever you found the book.

The gang and I are excited to see you in the next mystery adventure!

Fingers crossed there's nothing scary in that one...

Are You Afraid of the Dark?

Nyctophobia [nik-tuh-foh-bee-uh] is the intense and persistent fear of night or darkness. It comes from "nyktos," the Greek word for night, and "phóbos," the Greek word for fear.

Fear Rating: Nyctophobia is one of the most common phobias among children and to varying degrees adults. People with this phobia may experience dry mouth, dizziness, sweating, and panic attacks.

Origin: Fear of the dark may be caused by an instinctual survival response, a negative or traumatic past experience, and thoughts of hidden dangers.

Fear Facts:

- People with nyctophobia may have trouble sleeping, have panic attacks in dark places like the movies, and avoid leaving the house after dark.
- Some fear of the dark is natural, especially as a phase of child development.
- There is always some light, though humans may not be able to see it.
- Some beautiful things can only be seen in the dark, like the stars and moon.
- Tips: Set up a calm room, check for scary things, & think happy thoughts.

Jokes: Why is Dark spelled with a 'K' and not a 'C'?
Because you can't 'C' in the dark

Fear No More! With time and perspective, most can conquer the fear of darkness. But if you believe you suffer from nyctophobia and want help, talk to your parents or doctor about treatments. For more fear facts, visit: scaredybat.com/book6.

The mysterious adventures of Ellie Spark in

Scaredy Bat

Also by Marina J. Bowman:

The Legend of Pineapple Cove

To learn more, visit

scaredybat.com/book6

Don't miss
Book #7 in the

Scaredy Bat

series!

Learn more at:

scaredybat.com/book6next

Suspect List

Fill in the suspects as you read, and don't worry if they're different from Ellie's suspects. When you think you've solved the mystery, fill out the "who did it" section on the next page!

Name: Write the name of your suspect

Motive: Write the reason why your suspect might have committed the crime

Access: Write the time and place you think it could have happened

How: Write the way they could have done it

Clues: Write any observations that may support the motive, access, or how

Suspect 1

Draw below

Name:	
Motive:	
Access:	
How:	
Clues:	

Suspect 2

Draw below

Name:
Motive:
Access:
How:
Clues:

Suspect 3

Draw below

Name:	
Motive:	
Access:	
How:	
Clues:	

Suspect 4

Draw below

Name:	
Motive:	
Access:	
How:	
Clues:	

Who Did It?

Now that you've identified all of your suspects, it's time to use deductive reasoning to figure out who actually committed the crime! Remember, the suspect must have a strong desire to commit the crime (or cause the accident) and the ability to do so.

For more detective fun, visit:
scaredybat.com/book6

Name:	
Motive:	
Access:	
How:	
Clues:	

Hidden Details
Observation Sheet
-- Level One --

1. What game was Ellie playing when she was accidentally locked in the closet?

2. Who was the unknown caller on the phone?

3. What was Ellie afraid of at the beginning of the story?

4. What was the location of the mystery Ellie was asked to solve?

5. What was apparently stolen from the museum?

6. What is the troublesome Sam Thomlin?

7. What song did Fez play on the piano to open the secret door?

8. What did the kids find in the corner of the secret room?

9. What did Sam give Ellie in the basement?

10. Who was behind all the missing art and artifacts?

Hidden Details
Observation Sheet
-- Level Two --

1. How did Ellie get to the museum?

2. What fell when the museum alarm went off?

3. What did Tink and Carter use to test if the marble is real?

4. What was the fake ruby made of?

5. What did Fez drop that revealed the red laser beam?

6. What familiar object did Ellie notice painted in the mural?

7. Who grabbed Ellie's necklace in the secret room?

8. What did Ellie knock over when she fell through a secret wall chute?

9. Who was the surprise guest that Ellie's mom brought to the art show?

10. What special power does Ellie's necklace have?

Hidden Details
Observation Sheet
-- Level Three --

1. What does Ellie's mom use the attic for?

2. What is the name of the purple lemons on the museum tree sculpture?

3. Which museum room key supposedly went missing?

4. Who was the art curator?

5. What was the name of the black roses in the museum event room?

6. What was Clara planning to do after she retires from the museum?

7. What do the initials C.B. stand for?

8. What old fashioned device did Fez find in the secret room?

9. What kind of vehicle did Henry escape in?

10. What did Ellie's grandma give her to answer her questions about the necklace?

For more detective fun, visit:
scaredybat.com/book6

Answer Key

Level One Answers

1. Hide-and-seek
2. Henry Beagon
3. The dark
4. Brookside Vampire Artifact Museum
5. A painting
6. A ghost
7. Twinkle Twinkle Little Star
8. The missing painting and statue head
9. Her necklace
10. Henry Beagon

Level Two Answers

1. Bicycle
2. A sculpted marble head
3. Vinegar and a fork
4. Strawberry candy
5. A powdered donut hole
6. Her necklace
7. The ghost of Sam Thomlin
8. Knight armor
9. Grandma
10. It grants wishes

Level Three Answers

1. Art studio
2. Violem
3. Archive Room
4. Clara Burg
5. Bat Breath Roses
6. Cut hair
7. Charles Beagon
8. A camera
9. A white SUV
10. A journal that belonged to Grandpa Leo

128

Discussion Questions

1.   What did you enjoy about this book?

2.   What are some of the themes of this story?

3.   How did the characters use their strengths to solve the mystery together?

4.   What is your favorite museum and why?

5.   Have you ever been afraid of the dark?

6.   How did Ellie overcome her fear?

7.   If there was a secret passage in your house, where would it be?

8.   What other books, shows, or movies does this story remind you of?

9.   What do you think will happen in the next book in the series?

10. If you could talk to the author, what is one question you would ask her?

For more discussion questions, visit:
scaredybat.com/book6

129

About the Author

Marina J. Bowman is a writer and explorer who travels the world searching for wildly fantastical stories to share with her readers. Ever since she was a child, she has been fascinated with uncovering long lost secrets and chasing the mythical, magical, and supernatural. For her current story, Marina is investigating a charming town in the northern US, where vampires and humans live in harmony.

Marina enjoys sailing, flying, and nearly all other forms of transportation. She never strays far from the ocean for long, as it brings her both inspiration and peace. She stays away from the spotlight to maintain privacy and ensure the more unpleasant secrets she uncovers don't catch up with her.

As a matter of survival, Marina nearly always communicates with the public through her representative, Devin Cowick. Ms. Cowick is an entrepreneur who shares Marina's passion for travel and creative storytelling and is the co-founder of Code Pineapple.

Marina's last name is pronounced baumən, and rhymes with "now then."

Made in the USA
Middletown, DE
31 October 2022

13851158R00087